Straight Up!

Compilation Volume 1, Album Companion Book

For information contact: info@uptownmediaventures.com

Book and Cover design by Team Uptown

ISBN: 978-1-68121-043-8

First Edition: December 2016

10 9 8 7 6 5 4 3 2 1

Dedicated to Russell Atkins and Norman Jordan who were instrumental in the formation of the Muntu Poets.

To all the socially conscious literary minded poets, writers, musicians, painters, and all-around "cool cats."

Muntu

Derived from African Zulu culture that means a human being, sometimes used to mean "a Black person."

THE MUNTU POETS OF CLEVELAND
Muntu poets
the

Table of Contents

Foreword by Winston Gragg   7

Introduction   11

Mr. Gentleman aka C.E. Shy   13

    Biographical Information   14
    Literary Works   15

    The Second Wind   17
    Beauty Queen   19
    Escaped   21
    The Beast   23

Art Nixon   25

    Biographical Information   26
    Literary Works   28

    Highway Markers   29
    O.G.   33

Yaseen Assami   41

Biographical Information   42
Literary Works   43

A Glass of Lemonade   45
Bro-George Sista Kate   47

Yahya Abdussabur   49

Biographical Information   50
Literary Works   50

Clear Evidence   51
Dark Shadows   53

Elmer Buford   55

Biographical Information   56
Literary Works   57

We Are   59

Foreword

Like the tone and tenor when The Muntu Poets first arrived on the cultural and political scene of the turbulent mid '60s to the early '70s in the City of Cleveland, they have re-grouped over forty years later and are as relevant and provocative as ever. Their arrival on that scene was described in the introduction of *Muntu Poets Anthology Volume 2: 47 Years Later with Russell Atkins* - "They reflected the rage, dissent, and rebellious nature of the community during this time. The group consisted of several young members from every political stripe, from liberal to radical."

The group formed out of the leadership and tutelage of two exceptionally accomplished writer/poets: Russell Atkins and Norman Jordan. Russell Atkins, a major composer-editor-poet, used revolutionary musical structures in his writing, co-founding possibly the oldest black literary magazine in the country, *Freelance*, in 1950. Norman Jordan went on to become one of the most noted writers of the Black Arts Movement and have his work published in over 40 publications and plays performed internationally.

Four of the Muntu poets were in the movie *Uptight,* directed by Jules Dassin. Russell Atkins, Amir Rashidd, Yahya Abdussabur, and C.E. Shy. The movie was produced in 1968 in Cleveland, Ohio. Shortly after the film was released, the Glenville riots broke out.

The Muntu Poets' Volume 2 Anthology was a dedication to Russell Atkins and Norman Jordan and spearheaded by one of the original members of The Muntu Poets, C.E. Shy. Who knew that this would be the result of C.E. Shy contacting most of the original Muntu Poets and putting the proverbial "band and back together again," so to speak. Now we have the first Compilation CD Albums along with Companion Books for each volume. The Albums and the respective Companion Books of Collected Poems is named - what else - *Straight Up!* and *Ain't No Change!,* respectively.

There are reasons why I will cherish these Compilations and Companion Books. First off, the artistic effort that has come to fruition has its own value in the historical context of when and why The Muntu Poets came to exist. It was during a cataclysmic period in this country's Civil Rights struggle and the Black Arts Movement; and its re-discovery and intense identification with African History that deeply impacted the political awareness of the urban grassroots. Secondly, I get to savor the multifaceted beauty of both albums: These are poets who have matured yet definitely have NOT forgotten from whence they have come. These cats are now grandfathers, pillars of the community, one of them is even an active Imam.

The themes and moods range from angrily militant and political to heartbreakingly tender and romantic, to spiritual and fly old school *"lean & pull-a-chick" lyricisms.* The musical accompaniment ranges from Jazz, The Blues, Hip Hop, Classical and R&B.

Finally, these albums and their companion books are indeed trailblazers and will become more precious as the years progress. These "artifacts" are a witness to what a consciously evolved black man looks like having come of age during a period of riots, crime, poverty and, last but not least, a steadfast adherence to his muscular spirituality and artistic visions. I must say that these albums even one up the seminal 1970 album *The Last Poets*.

Completely accessible to both older and younger audiences, with a new millennium feel, that is trail blazing new artistic territory. Words cannot do these two classics justice which, to date, are unparalleled.

You will thoroughly enjoy these joints – *Straight Up!*

Winston Gragg
President
African American Music Association
Cleveland, Ohio

THE MUNTU POETS
ANTHOLOGY VOLUME 2

47 Years Later
With RUSSELL ATKINS

Introduction

The genesis of The Muntu Poets Legacy and Uptown Records occurred in a very unusual fashion. The Muntu Poets were in the process of publishing the anthology *Muntu Poets 47 Years later with Russell Atkins*, during the time frame in question.

To be honest, as the publisher of Uptown MJV Publishing, I was not paying much attention to the written works. I was in earnest attempting to collate all the poems, pictures and writer's bios into the nearly 200 page anthology.

One evening Mr. Gentleman, aka C.E. Shy, read a piece called *The Beast*. He read the passage with great emphasis and flair. I was floored!

"That has to be recorded!" I exclaimed.

That day was the genesis of Uptown MJV Records and, of course, the Muntu Poets Legacy. The process has been fraught with challenges but the end results (nearly 100 recordings of poetry with musical accompaniment) has been greatly rewarding!

Because many of the Muntu Poets are older and are located around the continental United States, some of the recordings were not done live in a studio. The Poets simply made recordings with whatever recording device available at their disposal. Many used their cell phones!

The end results have been surprisingly dramatic!

Also, there is a young clique, of poets, singers and rappers that is following in the footsteps of the Muntu Poets – the Legacies. They embody the resilient spirit and determination displayed by all the Muntu Poets from the 1960's onward.

The eclectic display of the multifaceted talents of the Muntu Poets is indeed fascinating. Enjoy!

K Kelly McElroy
Cleveland, Ohio

Mr. Gentleman aka C.E. Shy

Biographical Information

Mr. Gentleman aka C.E. Shy, an original Muntu Poet, has been writing since the seventh grade. He continued through high school, until he became more involved in sports. After graduating, he worked at the White Motors Company, where he was involved with the company's newspaper. He started a column called: "the Poets Corner." That was his first published work.

He moved to Sweden after he left the "States" with a one way ticket. He met an English photographer and started writing narratives, for some of the photographs that would be sold to newspapers and magazines.

After returning to the States, he joined a poetry workshop, the Muntu Poets, run by Russell Atkins and Norman Jordan from 1966 to 1968. He stopped writing for years, then started back writing again in late 1990's; when he started writing novellas and flash fiction, in addition to poetry. He joined a poetry workshop in Lyndhurst, Ohio at the county library in 2011 to hone his writing skills. He has been published in two anthologies and in the 60's in the Muntu Poets book of poems done by Russell Atkins and Norman Jordan.

Literary Works

Books

Substitutions
Time Share
Eclections 2
Eclections 3
Powhims and Proz
The House
Stories – The Long and the Short of It
Approaching the Ninth Dimension
Raw Forms, Structures and Vicissitudes
Me and Maysun
Deliver Me From Unconsciousness
The Visit
The Door at the End of the Hall
No U Turns One Way
Point Blank! Eclections 4
The Glimpse – A Remote View

Anthologies

The Muntu Poets of Cleveland Volume 1
Cuyahoga County Library Anthologies Volumes 1 - 4
The Muntu Poets 47 Years Later

Publications

White Motors

Substitutions
C.E. Shy
ECLECTIONS 2

Time Share
C.E. Shy
ECLECTIONS 3

WORDS IN THE
WIND
A BOOK OF POETIC PROSE BY
C.E SHY

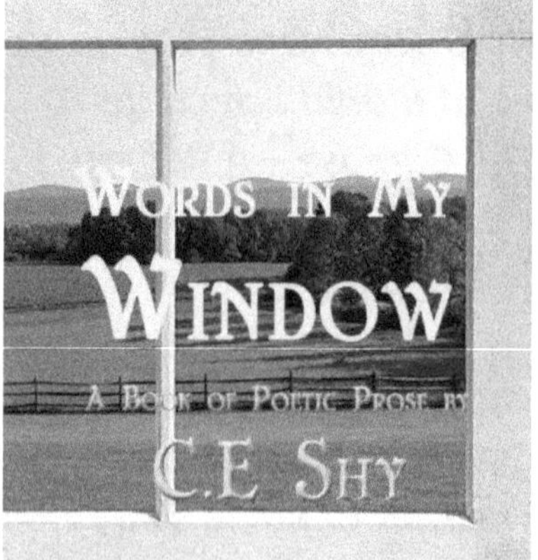

WORDS IN MY
WINDOW
A BOOK OF POETIC PROSE BY
C.E SHY

The Second Wind

Alarmed by my clock's passage of time
I craft these love letters with both
my hands.
Living in the shadows of my words
are photographs
of paragraphs of the emotions I
thought were gone.
As I lick a poem from your lips.
We dance with my
tongue in your cheek.

We duck windblown stones as
windows break around us.
My pen reluctantly releases the
verses that describe our affair.
 Unkind magic attempts to interfere.
It was no match for sincere intentions.
The sidewalk held the stories of foot steps
The lawn collected what the rain rinsed.
The climate changed in my face.
But the kite that we lost was returned to us by
the second wind.

C. E.
SHY

THE
HOUSE
C.E. SHY

STORIES
THE LONG AND
THE SHORT OF IT
C.E.
SHY
ARMCHAIR
CHRONICLES
ME AND
MAYSUN
C.E. SHY
WITH
MAYSUN SHAHEED

Beauty Queen

So you are the girl in the magazine!
Under your picture reads, "Beauty Queen"
Yes that's you there is no mistake!

I've met you at last for goodness sake!
Now what's your name I've rather forgotten
You see my memory for name is quite rotten.

I have waited for years to ask you to dance
If you don't mind giving this chance. You are far more
Beautiful than your pictures reveal.

Looks like your man has got himself a good deal..
I have all of your photos at home on my shelf.
 Sometimes for hours you're mine to myself.

 Ahh ...That frown on your forehead that I despise.
It takes the mystery out of your eyes.
Thanks for the dance I said with a grin.
Before I leave... what's your name again?

Approaching
The Ninth
Deminsion
C.E.
Shy

Deliver
Me From
Un
conscious
ness

C.E.
Shy

Raw Forms,
Structures and
Vicissitudes of
the
Neighborhood
C.E.
Shy

THE
VISIT
PASSPORT
C.E.
Shy

Escaped

Another step closer I couldn't have gotten away.
Another step closer I would have wanted to stay.
Another step closer I would not have heard the warning.
Another step closer I couldn't have left in the morning.
Another step closer I wouldn't have made a good choice.
Another step closer I couldn't have resisted your voice.
Another step closer I would have been enthralled by
your charms.
Another step closer, I'd be locked in your arms.
Another step closer I would have listened to my heart
instead of my mind.
And in direction I'm traveling I couldn't afford to be
blind.
Another step closer I would have lost the race,
never again to escape your embrace.
The warmth a body I never did touch.
The kiss of your lips I wanted so much.
As I came closer to the end of my expression,
I am nowhere near the end of my passion
I'm nowhere near the end of my desire.
First things first...I'm afraid of the fire

Four of the Muntu poets were in the movie *Uptight,*
directed by Jules Dassin: Russell Atkins, Amir Rashidd,
Yahya Abdussabur, and C.E. Shy.

The movie was made in Cleveland, Ohio 1968.
Shortly after the film was released, the Glenville Riots
broke out.

The Beast

(Written by Amirr Rashidd)

Beneath the tall and shadowy trees
My brother black danced with ease
And yet the morning brought disaster
The beast is coming faster, faster.

My brothers black withheld their pride
They went so far as suicide
They surely knew that death held no pains
The beast is coming with shackling chains.

He burned my farm and slashed my arm
And brought me far from home
Across the sea to the land of the free
The beast is coming to burn your home.

The beast said we were ignorant
Said we were totally incompetent
Yes, we won his wars and grew his crops
The beast is coming, your freedom to stop.

Brothers black please hear the cry
Our mothers weep, our fathers sigh
Black men brothers black we're free
Let's fight and die for land you see.

War with the beast, it must be won
The task of fate has now begun
We must strike with such great pain

So that the beast will never rise again.
Brothers black all free men cry
We've won our life through endless plights
Brothers black walk without sigh
The beast is dead, hear freedom cry.

Art Nixon

Biographical Information

Art Nixon, living in the Los Feliz Village District of Los Angeles, California, became interested in writing after being introduced to poetry as a member of the Muntu Poets of Cleveland writing workshop headed by Russell Atkins. He wrote and performed his poetry as a member of the Muntu Poets, eventually performing his poetry with various poetry groups locally, at colleges, around the state, and on area radio stations. His interest in writing led him to write essays and poetry for *Black Ascensions* literary and was one of four founders/editors which included Anthony fudge, Larry Howard, and Larry Wade [RIP] in the early 70s. The magazine was a first for Cuyahoga Community College and went on to earn honorable mention for college magazines in *Essence Magazine.*

A Cum Laude Graduate of Case Western Reserve University while married with a 3 year old son, he brought the child to class frequently when babysitters weren't available. [His son is now a professor at a major Los Angeles University with two award winning books and a third just published, "Race On The QT: Blackness in The Films of Quentin Tarantino," University of Texas Press]. Nixon published papers in Academic Journals as an undergraduate, while employed as a module tutor/instructor at Cuyahoga Community College's writing Lab. He also was employed as a visiting Poet-At-Large for the Cleveland Area Arts Council, introducing Greater Cleveland high school, middle school and elementary students to the first celebrated African American poets as early as 18th century slaves Phyllis Wheatley and Juniper Harmon, the Harlem Renaissance writers to those of contemporary urban poetry.

In Los Angeles, Nixon worked as a security guard for many years while writing screenplays, plays, and TV pilots, none of which he was able to get produced. He also wrote a weekly column for now defunct Las Vegas and Los Angeles black focused newspapers, Bronze News and Balance News for several years. He has been published in several poetry anthologies, including *Black American Literature Forum, The Drumming Between Us, Catch The Fire: A Cross-Generational Anthology of African American Poetry,* along with several other works.

He is included in Columbia Granger's Index of African American Poets. Currently, he is working on the novelization of one of his screenplays. It was published as a short story in Robert Fleming's anthology of short stories, *Too Much Boogie: Erotic Remixes of The Dirty Blues*. He has two sons and two grandkids. He is recently retired as front desk manager at The Beverly Hilton Hotel.

Literary Works

<u>Anthologies</u>

The Muntu Poets of Cleveland Volume 1
Black American Literature Forum
The Drumming Between Us
Catch The Fire: A Cross-Generational Anthology of
        African American Poetry
Voices from Leimert Park: a poetry anthology
Too Much Boogie: Erotic Remixes of The Dirty Blues
The Muntu Poets 47 Years Later with Russell Atkins

Highway Markers,
Review Mirrors
(For Cheryl)

Inside the car
In the mirror
The sky has just dissolved a red tablet of sun
And dyed itself   hot pink   maroon
And   now, black.

Mute and rejected & filed at less than mile intervals
The highway markers sprout in the headlight spray
And wither red in the taillights passing.
The Truth Is:
In the beginning was the end.
Even
The
Orgasm
Begins in a thin wheeze of need,
But soon becomes
A glorious megaphone
Announcing its own
Departure

Even
The
Mystics have sometimes taught there is a death
After life after death...

The shoe presses down and the markers rush up
To the windows like obedient phantoms
Where you see them for what they are:
Cheap fixtures to be jettisoned from
The night-long room,
Flash passed and gulped up by the blackness
Leaning full-blown and immovable
All across the car's rear view:
Each beginning existing at the mercy of an ending.

It is what it means
To see chunks
Of highway night-space
After each marker that is passed.
It is what someone said
They thought you should have been;
And *more* than you knew yourself to be,
It is what it means to have been legally in love.

The highway markers will parade infinity
Across one more state line
Before the night begins to nod,
It's last cup of strong black coffee
loosened from its fingers
And spills onto the asphalt in an
Obscene libation:
Finally, the night,
Supine in the middle of
The highway, shoe-less,
Dirty sock soles on one foot

And the other barefoot,
Will lay with its mouth gaped bright blue.

From time   to   time   it is
The rear view that is viewed and reviewed
That   mirrors   the   wall of black
You've been speeding through,
With not a trace to betray your direction.
 From   time   to   time until
The Light: the eyes will check.
They *know* there can be
New beginnings   but seem   to   need   more proof,
That you've been
Where you've been

--Art Nixon/1977

Art Nixon is a contributing writer in *Catch the Fire!!! A Cross-Generational Anthology of Contemporary African-American Poetry*

O.G.
(For Alexis N.)

Eternal Ace-Boons

arms linked arm-in arm

in lock-step

since time without beginning--

even before this planet had a spot

to spin on

we exchanged these Bodhisattva rings,

we shared and we share

this Buddha thing:

Sho-i-sho Nyo ze so

Nyo ze sho   Nyo ze Tai

Nyo ze riki   Nyo ze sa

Nyo ze in   Nyo ze en

Nyo ze ka   Nyo ze ho

Nyo ze honmak^kukyo---My G!!!

Some lifetimes she's been my *Sensei*

and I her assigned hand servant,

she's been my mama,

my daughter

my husband

She's been my dog and me hers,

my muse, my distraction, my disciple

We've been bitter cellmates sentenced to

the same hermaphroditic shell

in at least a couple of lifetimes,

arguing, bickering who try'n to catch

who up in the clubs all the way back

to them secret palm wine spots in plain

view of the Serengeti & Bacchanalia

backrooms

Musta been something I did this last time

'cause it took me half this lifetime

to catch up with you this time

in this city of angels and demons

Didn't fool me. I read the clues:

same initials we share. Same North Side, Pittsburgh
birthplace.

read the Lotus sutra in your eyes. Straight-up *Knew*
who you was

despite your having gone behind my back,

cashed-in a fist-full of *my* karmic bonus points

and showed up in *this* lifetime

as out-of-control gorgeous with nutmeg for freckles

and that beast-taming grin:

Yeah, that's right--straight up recognized ya!

Talk'n shit. Exhaling Virginia Slims out the corner of
your mouth,

slipping compassion like bidness cards

to grimy souls on the QT,

trolling and strolling

that furry pet you secretly

told me you called "Big Mystic" on

a short leash & wearing your trademark

silk boxers--MY *G!!*

My *G!!*

My Ms black Dickies work pants wearing

Dap-Daddy. Double butch-down. Dudette.

Strapped in with suspenders and no nonsense shoes,

Porkpie broke way down

over the eyes--not for affect--but as a private partition

for strong & direct eye contact

before she gets all up in my head

all up in my head,

she's a Buddha Gangster

in a slit evening gown and slut-pumps: *working it!*

her gown riding upper thigh high and not in the least
self-conscious

with pumps kicked off for more grip: *gone work this!*

Gone git to the bottom of this,

Gone thug some enlightenment up out

The steel compartments of my self-delusions and

Half-ass perpetrations, Gone make Ugly Truths

Rise...Rise...RISE...big-bitch-on-up outta there...

And waddle casually across the floor where I'm living

We share the laughter of punch lines

to jokes we made up thousands of lifetimes ago

We move in and out

and around and thru each other's spirit

as though they were second homes

And sleep deeply and well

because we found out: *Again,*

In this lifetime,

Who's got

Our

Back

-Art Nixon 2006

Art Nixon is a contributing writer in the *Voices from Leimert Park: a poetry anthology*

The Original Muntu Poets workshop located on the 2nd floor at the intersection of Ansel Road and Superior Avenue, Cleveland, Ohio.
(Photo credit: Yaseen A. Assami)

Yaseen Assami

Biographical Information

Yaseen Assami , aka Perry Wesley Davis, was born on November 12, 1948 in Knoxville, Tennessee. After high school he moved to Cleveland, Ohio.

Here he met several of his long-time friends and Russell Atkins. He, subsequently, became a part of the Muntu Poets. His stay with the Muntu Poets was of short duration but his involvement was very influential and an important part of his development as a youth and a young expressionist writer. Assami counts Russell Atkins as a very good friend and a mentor; a person of unparalleled talent and creative ability. He counts his association with Russell Atkins as an honor. He also has valued relationships with other writers and poets who feel the same esteem for the inspiring literary figure.

Literary Works

<u>Books</u>

From Realism to Surrealism

<u>Anthologies</u>

The Muntu Poets of Cleveland Volume 1
Cuyahoga County Library Anthologies Volumes 1 - 4
The Muntu Poets 47 Years Later with Russell Atkins

FROM
REALISM
TO SURREALISM
A BOOK OF POETIC PROSE
BY
YASEEN
ASSAMI
THE BROWN PAPER BAG BLUES...

A Glass of Lemonade

Oh just a glass of lemonade.
I would snatch the tear drops from your eyes
And rip the love from your heart.
Oh for a glass of lemonade.
I would wade through oceans of blood,
And kill the meaning of desire.
I love you more than sunshine,
But less than moonlight,
And lemonade.
Sometimes I find myself crawling through nightmares
Only to be saved by a glass of lemonade.
Tyme snatches the chill from the refridgerator .
My shadow stands shivering screaming for a glass Of
lemonade,
I set at the table talking to my former tymes.
Watching tomorrow make love to a glass of lemonade.
Wandering through Charlie's mind.
Kicking over trash cans of ideals, burning
Old newspapers.
Terror trembles in the path of death.
Fate hides behind yesterday's excuses,
Watching angry butterflies fling grenades at dead horses.
While drinking a glass of lemonade
Observing paper progenies play chubby in piles of
broken hearts.
Bowls.bells.Birds sing songs of joy
I sit wondering why love wears a mask of lunacy.

Running through a blues song canoodling camels.
Waving goodbye to insanity,
Drinking a glass of lemonade.

Bro-George Sista-Kate

Doo doo wap is strong in here i have no idea where i
have been or where i might go .last
tyme i checked i was headed toward snowstorm in a
landslide pushed down a hill by a
lightning strike putting a 20 on a 10 calling on a reason to
work my way past the struggle
and strife of a tyme when life's long empty song of pain
and suffering was the norm.
Paying for water i can not drink Do Doo Wap is strong in
here.
hoping for a dream that can turn nightmares into a joyful
life Doo Doo Wap is strong
in HERE
WELL WELL WELL the smell of the trees and the whine of
misery.
Ripps my mind away from the joy of a SADDDD winter
Song
about a season filled with the gentle caresses of a
COLORED FELLAS effort
to escape the abstract reality of HIS STORY.
DOO DO WAP is Strong in here.
BROTHER GEORGE AND SISTER KATE stand holding hands
as i leave out the
door chasing the dream of a deal that will never close.
DO DO WAPP IS STRONG OUT
HERE

Russell Atkins with members of the Writers Workshop (John Donoghue, Bob Donoghue, John Stickneyam, and Faheem Khabeer (sitting far left)); and some members of the Original Muntu Poets including: Norman Jordan (standing 2nd from left), C.E. Shy (standing 4th from left), Yaseen A. Assami (standing last from left), and Yahya Abdussabur (sitting last from left)
(Photo credit: Diane Kendig)

Yahya Abdussabur

Biographical Information

Yahya Abdussabur/nee (Jon Hall) was born August 11, 1943 in Cleveland Ohio. In 1967, after reading the autobiography of Malcolm X and the Black Nationalist movement, he sought to express this awareness. He was invited to attend a writers' workshop at the opportunities industrialization center, which was located on intersection of Superior Avenue and Ansel Road.

On attending, he was impressed by the black men there and their ability to express themselves by spoken word. He was so impressed that he went home and composed a few poems. This resulted in his being a part of the workshop effort which took the name the Muntu Poets. His membership in the group led to his exposure to a bigger world and to his becoming a devout devotee of Islam that is practiced all over the world.

Literary Works

Anthologies

The Muntu Poets of Cleveland Volume 1
New Black Poetry
The Muntu Poets 47 Years Later with Russell Atkins

Clear Evidence

in the name of Allah, Most Gracious, Most Merciful

it is a matter of faith
that brings about the
fact of the matter
faith put into practice
which brings about change

methods of conduct which eradicate
barriers of ignorance
resulting in states
of concern, manners of
redress--hope based
on clear evidence
clear evidence
of the morning light
which follows the
darkness of deprivation
the clear evidence illustrated
by the flowers
the bloom in the field
once bare of herbage

Yahya Abdussabur is a contributing writer in the *New Black Poetry* anthology

Dark Shadows

          dark shadows
                  move into confronted
camps
              instant dismay
      to the chosen few
      what is the wind
that produces such?
      what is the meaning
of this omen?
        in structure,
this substance
          seems the
same
    unproportionate
disagreement on
  its name---
            seeds lie
wasted on
    unproductive soil
    no one toils
the earth
              barren thorns
                  catch minds
and leave them as
    evidence of
                chaotic times

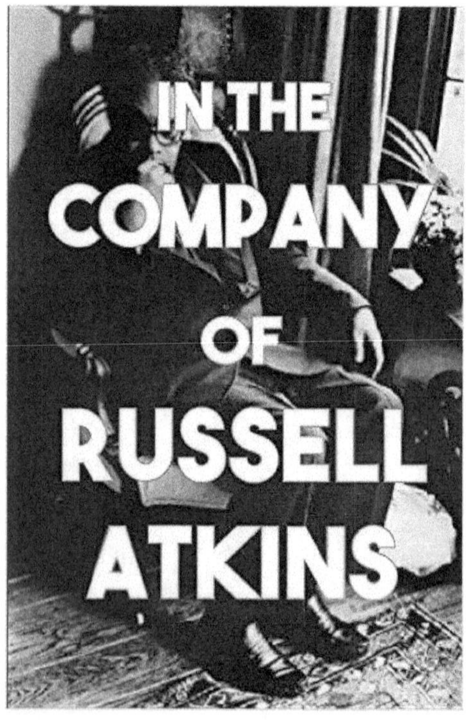

Russell Atkins (center sitting) at the *In The Company of Russell Atkins* book launch along with Mr. Gentleman (sitting left), Yaseen Assami, Bob McDonough, Elmer Buford (standing left to right), and John Donoghue (sitting right).

Elmer Buford

Biographical Information

Elmer Buford, an original Muntu Poet, was born in Cleveland, Ohio on May 2, 1933. He served in the U.S. Army in Korea and Japan. After his honorable discharge in December, 1955, he took courses at Cuyahoga Community College and Cleveland State University, where he eventually received associate and bachelor degrees respectively.

He authored and published a book named *Conclusions* in 1971 under the pen name B. Felton. Russell Atkins himself wrote the forward for this book. Gaining widespread literary recognition, Buford has been published in the *Broadside Press* (Detroit, Michigan), the *Free Lance*, the *Muntu Journal*, the *Sattvas Review*, the *Vindicator, the Cleveland Record*, and other publications.

Literary Works

Books

Conclusions

Anthologies

The Muntu Poets of Cleveland Volume 1
The Muntu Poets 47 Years Later with Russell Atkins

Publications

The Broadside Press
The Free Lance
The Muntu Journal
The Sattvas Review
The Cleveland Record

Published 1971, authored by B Felton (aka Elmer
Buford), forward by Russell Atkins

We Are

We are what/
           We are – that
We are sometimes/
           More other times
Less – we are/
           What might've been
But never occurred/
           We are not
The occurring experience/
           Of a whole
Or particular manifestation/
           That was thought
Too have been.../
           We are truly
The ingrates of/
           Flesh-sweat-blood
And tears-the/
           Mariners-renegades
Castaways-all we/
           Are-the consoled
Triumphs & disasters/
           That border on
Fear-domination-jealousy/
           Violence insecurity
Imbeciles of mediocrity/
           Genius of love
The deprived-the/
           Depraved with insatiable
Appetites full of/

                    Ghastly horrors that
That know end…/
                    We are the
Plunderers-pimps-queens/
                    Bitches-punks-whores
& castaways split/
                    Up to regroup
Mightier than before/
                    We are the
Earth's inheritance &/
                    It will inherit
We – we are/
                    That we are…

                    Elmer Buford aka B. Felton
                    June 14, 1970

THE UNSUNG MASTERS SERIES
RUSSELL ATKINS
On the Life & Work of an American Master
Edited by Kevin Prufer & Michael Dumanis

Russell Atkins reviews recent poetry By Muntu Poet
C.E. Shy, aka Mr. Gentleman
(Photo Credit: C.E. Shy 2015)

Norman Jordan was an internationally known poet who made his home in Fayette County, West Virginia. Jordan, pictured here in the African American Heritage Family Tree Museum which he founded in Ansted, West Virginia, was also well-known for his portrayal of figures such as Carter G. Woodson and as a playwright and arts administrator.

Norman Jordan was a member of the Griot Collective Poetry Workshop of Jackson, Tennessee. In 2008, he became an official member of the Affrilachian Poets of Lexington, Kentucky.

Straight Up!

Compilation Volume 1, Album Companion Book

UPTOWN
MEDIA JOINT VENTURES
PUBLISHING

UPTOWN
MEDIA JOINT VENTURES
RECORDS

www.ingramcontent.com/pod-product-compliance
Lightning Source LLC
Chambersburg PA
CBHW071509030726

47593CB00003B/1227